Thumbelina

THE WORLD'S SMALLEST HORSE

By Kristen L. Depken
Photographs by Austin Hargrave and Goose Creek Farms

A Random House PICTUREBACK® Book

Random House New York

 Published in the United States by Random House Children's Books, a division of Random House, Inc., 1745 Broadway, New York, NY 10019, in conjunction with Thumbelina Enterprises, LLC.

Library of Congress Control Number: 2010933163
ISBN: 978-0-375-86355-4
randomhouse.com/kids
Printed in the United States of America
10 9 8 7 6 5 4 3 2

Meet Thumbelina, the world's smallest horse! Don't let her size fool you—Thumbelina may be tiny, but she has a very big heart.

Thumbelina is a dwarf miniature horse. Most miniature horses are two to three feet tall. But because she's also a dwarf, Thumbelina is only one and a half feet tall, and she weighs just fifty-seven pounds.

Regular-sized horses stand about five to six feet tall and can weigh over a thousand pounds—that's the equivalent of almost twenty Thumbelinas!

Thumbelina was born on May 1, 2001, at Goose Creek Farms, a miniature-horse farm in St. Louis, Missouri.

Most newborn miniature horses are about eighteen inches tall and weigh around twenty pounds. Baby Thumbelina stood only ten inches tall and weighed just eight and a half pounds. That's smaller than many human babies!

When she was a newborn, Thumbelina's tiny size made it difficult for her to reach up to drink her mother's milk. But with help and lots of hard work, she grew strong and healthy.

Today, Thumbelina is a healthy eater. For breakfast and lunch each day, she has one cup of oats and a handful of hay. This is not as much as other horses eat, but it's plenty for Thumbelina! She also likes to graze on grass and snack on apples and carrots.

Like many dwarf miniature horses, Thumbelina was born with crooked legs that made it difficult for her to walk—until she got a pair of very special shoes from her farrier.

A farrier is a person who takes care of a horse's hooves. Thumbelina's farrier visits her regularly. He makes sure that her shoes fit well and that it's comfortable for her to walk, run, and play.

Just like other horses, Thumbelina is groomed every day. This means that her dark brown coat is brushed to keep it smooth and shiny. She also takes a bath with a hose sometimes—but she does *not* like it!

In the winter, Thumbelina's coat grows long and shaggy to keep her warm. The coat is shed in the summer so that she can stay cool.

Despite her small size, Thumbelina is a natural leader. She has been known to boss around all the other horses on the farm—even the biggest ones!

Thumbelina gets along with lots of other animals, too—especially dogs!

Thumbelina's very best friend is a dog named Cassie. They love to play in the fields and explore the farm together. Cassie watches out for Thumbelina, barking if she senses danger. No matter where Cassie goes, Thumbelina likes to be right by her side.

One day, Thumbelina decided that she wanted to sleep in Cassie's doghouse—and Cassie didn't mind! Now Thumbelina spends every night in the doghouse instead of in her stall, with Cassie camped right outside.

Every year, Thumbelina hops in the ThumbyMobile, a tour bus with her own private stall in the back. She spends several months visiting sick and needy children around the country.

Thumbelina loves to meet kids—and they love meeting her! She brings them comfort when they are feeling sad or lonely, and shows them that their differences can make them special, just like her.

While traveling, Thumbelina likes to take a break and see the sights. She's been to forty-eight states and has visited Niagara Falls, the Grand Canyon, Mount Rushmore, and even the White House!

But Thumbelina's most important job is sharing love and joy with those who need it most—and showing everyone that being small doesn't mean you can't do great things.